MATERIAL WORLD

# STATES OF MATTER

**Robert Snedden**

**Chicago, Illinois**

Customer Service  888-454-2279
Visit our website at www.heinemannraintree.com

Designed by Victoria Bevan and Q2A Solutions
Printed and bound in China, by South China Printing Co. Ltd.

12 11 10 09 08
10 9 8 7 6 5 4 3 2 1

New edition ISBNs:    1-4329-0096-X (hardcover)
                      1-4329-0101-X (paperback)
13-digit ISBNs:   978-1-4329-0096-0 (hardcover)
                  978-1-4329-0101-1 (paperback)

**The Library of Congress has cataloged the first edition as follows:**
Snedden, Robert.
    States of matter / Robert Snedden.
       p. cm. – (Material world)
    Includes bibliographical references and index.
    ISBN 1-58810-072-3 (library binding)
    1. Matter–Properties–Juvenile literature. [1. Matter–Properties.] I. Title.

QC173.16 .S54  2001
530.4–dc21

                                                    00-061345

**Acknowledgments**
The publishers would like to thank the following for permission to reproduce photographs: Bruce Coleman
Collection pp. **11** (Dr. Eckart Pott), **24** (Stephen J. Krasemann); FLPA p. **21** (M. J. Thomas); John Cleare p. **22**;
Network p. **14** (Peter Jordan); Photolibrary p. **7** (Digital Vision); Science Photo Library pp. **4** (NASA), **9** (Dr.
Jeremy Burgess), **10** (Tony Craddock), **16** (Angela Murphy), **19**, **29** (Simon Terrey); Telegraph Colour Library
p. **13** (Chris Simpson); Tony Stone Images pp. **15** (Greg Pease), **18** (Randy Wells), **20** (David Madison),
**23** (J. Sneesby/B. Wilkins).

Cover photograph of test tubes reproduced with permission of Masterfile.

# Contents

Some words are shown in bold, **like this**. You can find out what they mean by looking in the glossary.

# What Is Matter?

Matter is all around us. Everything that you see, touch, feel, smell, or taste is made of matter. The Sun in the sky, the hair on your head, and the scent of a cake in the oven are all forms of matter. Matter is anything that takes up space—whether it be a spinning galaxy of stars or the tiny speck of an **atom**.

A space-walking astronaut may not feel the effects of gravity, but he still has the same mass as he does on Earth.

## Mass and gravity

One feature that all objects possess is **mass**. The mass of an object is the amount of matter it contains. Mass is not the same as weight. The weight of an object is the effect of the force of **gravity** on the object's mass. The mass always stays the same, but the weight can increase or decrease depending on how strong the force of gravity is on the object.

Every object is attracted to every other object by the force of gravity. The greater the mass of an object, the greater the gravitational force it exerts. Earth has a much greater mass than you, and so your weight is actually a measurement of Earth's gravitational force acting on your mass.

# Particles of matter

All materials are made of atoms, which in turn are made of even smaller **particles** called **protons, neutrons**, and **electrons**. Scientists have worked hard to find the tiniest building blocks of matter—the particles from which all the materials we know are made. The study of the particles that make up everything is called particle **physics**.

**Atoms of different elements can link together in a variety of ways to form compounds.**

Ionic bond

Sodium ion

Chlorine ion

# Atoms, elements, and molecules

Atoms can join together to form larger particles called **molecules**. Molecules are the smallest particles of an **element** or **compound** that can exist on their own without being joined to other atoms or groups of atoms. Hydrogen atoms, for example, are not found on their own. They are joined together in pairs to form hydrogen molecules. Molecules that contain atoms of one kind only are known as elements; those that contain atoms of different kinds are called compounds. Molecules vary in size from the hydrogen molecule (which is made up of two hydrogen atoms, the smallest atoms) to the complex **macromolecules** of proteins (which are essential in all living things and can contain many thousands of atoms).

# Changing States

Matter usually exists in one of three forms, or states: solid, liquid, or gas. The state depends on how freely the particles that make up the matter can move around. Most of the substances we come across will be in one of these states. Water is a good example of a substance that can be found in all three states in everyday circumstances—as solid ice in a freezer, running water from a tap, and steam rising from a boiling kettle.

The changes from one state to another take place at definite temperatures called the melting point (solid to liquid) and the boiling point (liquid to gas). Changes in the opposite direction are brought about by cooling as a gas condenses to form a liquid or as a liquid freezes to form a solid.

## TRY IT YOURSELF

**You will need:**
vinegar
baking soda
small plastic bottle
saucepan
spoon
balloon

**Can a solid and a liquid combine to create a gas?**

1  Have an adult warm the vinegar in a saucepan and pour it into the bottle until it is about a quarter full.
2  Put one spoonful of baking soda into the balloon.
3  While holding the balloon carefully, so that the baking soda does not fall out, stretch the neck of the balloon over the neck of the bottle.
4  Quickly lift the balloon so that the baking soda spills into the vinegar.

The vinegar and the baking soda will react together to produce carbon dioxide gas. As this happens, the balloon starts to inflate, which shows that a gas takes up a greater **volume** than the same amount of a solid or a liquid.

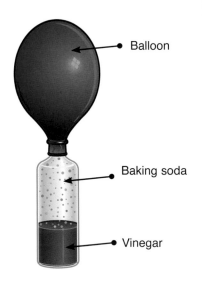

Balloon

Baking soda

Vinegar

## Latent heat

A substance can be changed from one state to another by raising or lowering its temperature. The heat absorbed by a substance as it changes state (for example, from a solid to a liquid) or the heat that is released by it (from a gas to a liquid) is called the **latent heat** of the substance.

When a solid changes to a liquid, heat is taken in. When the liquid changes back to a solid, the same amount of heat is given out. This is called the latent heat of **fusion**. The amount of heat required to change a liquid into a gas is called the latent heat of **vaporization.**

## Sublimation

**Sublimation** is an unusual change of state in which a solid changes directly into a gas without first becoming a liquid. For example, solid carbon dioxide (sometimes called dry ice) sublimes to carbon dioxide gas. When the gas is cooled, it becomes a solid again.

Solid carbon dioxide (dry ice) is often used to create smoke effects on stage as it turns into a gas.

# Solids

Solids are matter in a form that has a definite shape and volume. The volume of a material is the amount of space it takes up. The atoms that make up a solid are not free to move around like they are in a liquid or a gas.

Solid objects, such as stone, are rigid and hard and will keep their shape unless a physical force acts on them to change it. Some solids are **brittle** and will shatter when struck. Metals are malleable (they can be beaten into thin sheets) and ductile (they can be drawn out into wires). The properties of a solid depend on the particles that make up the substance and the forces acting among them. The atoms in almost all solids are arranged in regular patterns called **crystals**.

### A supercooled liquid

Glass is sometimes called a supercooled liquid. It softens easily when heated and has no definite melting point like true solids. Unlike a true solid, the particles that make up glass can move around, although very slowly. Over long periods, glass can "flow" like a liquid. The effect can be seen in very old windows in which the glass is thicker at the bottom than at the top.

GAS

LIQUID

SOLID

The atoms in a solid are not free to move. They are held in place by the forces that bind them together.

# Bonding together

The tightly packed particles that make up a solid are held together by chemical **bonds**. These are the forces of attraction that hold together atoms of one or more type of element to form molecules. The main types of bonding are **ionic** and **covalent**. The type of bond formed depends on the elements that bond together.

In ionic bonds, the combining atoms gain or lose electrons to become **ions**. For example, in sodium chloride (salt), a sodium atom loses an electron to form a sodium ion, while a chlorine atom gains an electron to form a chloride ion. Strong electrical forces hold the oppositely **charged** ions together. When covalent bonds are formed, the outer electrons of two atoms overlap and so are effectively shared between the two atoms.

The particles in a solid such as a salt crystal are held together in regular patterns.

# Melting

The molecules that make up a solid are arranged so that the forces that attract and repel the molecules are evenly balanced. The molecules do not have enough energy to move to different parts of the solid, but vibrate around these positions of balance. If the temperature of a solid is raised, the molecules begin to vibrate more strongly. Eventually the vibrations become great enough to overcome the forces that hold the molecules in place. When this happens, the solid melts and becomes a liquid.

# Liquids

A liquid is similar to a solid because it has a definite volume. However, the molecules that make up a liquid do not have fixed positions as they do in a solid, and they are further apart than in a solid. A liquid is similar to a gas because its molecules are not fixed to each other in any particular way. The molecules in a liquid are able to move short distances, but they do not have the freedom of movement found in the molecules that make up a gas.

Liquids and gases are both called **fluids** because they can flow to fit the shape of any container into which they are put. The molecules of a liquid will always follow the shape of their container, but they will not spread out in all directions to fill it.

If liquids are heated beyond a certain point, they change into gas. This is called boiling—for example, boiling water changes into steam. If liquids are cooled below a certain point, they change into solids—for example, water freezes into ice. Different liquids have different freezing and boiling points.

Liquids take on the shape of any container into which they are poured.

## Surface tension

Attractive forces between water molecules create a skin-like barrier between the air and the water. This is called **surface tension**. Some insects can walk on this water "skin."

# Capillary action

**Capillary** action is the tendency of liquids to move into or out of thin tubes called capillaries. It occurs whenever a liquid in a capillary is in contact with the air. Surface tension draws liquid into a capillary if the nearby capillary walls strongly attract the molecules of the liquid's surface. On the other hand, surface tension will push liquid out of a capillary if the liquid molecules are more strongly attracted to each other than to the capillary walls.

Capillary action draws water up the roots of plants. Paper towels have millions of capillaries between their fibers that absorb water by capillary action.

Surface tension enables a water beetle to walk across the surface of a pond without sinking.

## TRY IT YOURSELF

**You will need:**

water

4 wooden toothpicks

liquid dish soap

shallow dish

dropper

**Are toothpicks drawn toward or away from surface tension?**

1 Put some water in a shallow dish and wait until the surface is smooth.

2 Carefully float the toothpicks on the surface together so that they are all pointing inward.

3 Using a dropper, gently put a drop of liquid dish soap in the middle of the dish between the toothpicks.

The surface tension in the center is broken by the liquid dish soap, and the toothpicks immediately move out toward the rim of the dish, drawn by the surface tension on the water there.

# Gases

Gas is a form of matter in which the molecules are free to move around randomly in otherwise empty space. A gas, such as the air that surrounds us, has neither a fixed shape nor a fixed volume. It will spread out to fill any size or shape of container into which it is put. All gases, whatever the molecules are that make them up, will behave in the same way.

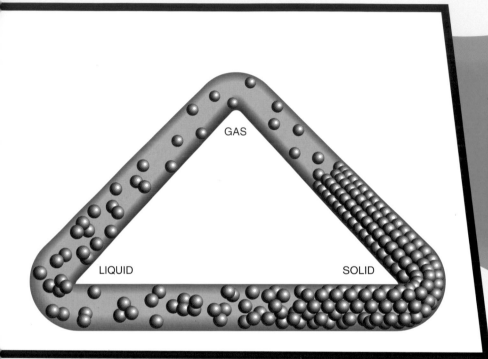

GAS

LIQUID

SOLID

**The molecules that make up a gas are not bound together and move around randomly in all directions.**

Although you may not be able to see them, gases have weight just like solids and liquids. Because the particles that make up a gas are spread out thinly, a volume of gas under normal conditions will contain fewer particles and so weigh less than the same volume of a solid or liquid in which the particles are more tightly packed together.

## In the air

Every cubic inch of air contains many billions of molecules all moving around rapidly. These gas particles are so small that they occupy only about one-thousandth of that cubic inch. The remaining space between the gas particles is empty. The speed at which the gas particles move is determined by their weight and by the temperature of the gas. Light particles move faster than heavy ones, and the hotter the gas the faster the particles move. The gas particles are constantly colliding with each other and with the walls of any container they happen to be in. These collisions produce the effect of **pressure**.

# Gases and liquids

A gas changes to a liquid when it is cooled enough for the gas particles to gather together. This is because the drop in temperature lowers the speed of the molecules and so enables attractive forces between them to bind them together. The temperature at which a gas becomes a liquid is called its **condensation point**. If the pressure of the gas is increased, it will become a liquid at a higher temperature as the particles are forced closer together, allowing the attractive forces to work.

## Gas laws

Gases behave according to three rules, or laws, that explain how the pressure, temperature, volume, and the number of particles in a container of gas are related.

- Boyle's law says that the pressure of a gas increases as the volume of the gas decreases. If you shrink a container full of gas, the pressure of the gas in that container will increase. If you squeeze a balloon, you can feel the pressure of the gas inside it resisting your squeeze.

- Charles's law says that a gas expands at a constant rate as its temperature rises. For example, doubling the temperature doubles the gas's volume, as long as the pressure does not change. The law was developed by French scientists and hot-air ballooners Jacques Charles and Joseph Gay-Lussac in the 1780s. Heating air in a balloon causes its volume to increase and its density to decrease, making it lighter than the surrounding air.

- Avogadro's law says that equal volumes of different gases all contain the same number of particles if they all have the same pressure and temperature.

The bubbles from this diver's breathing apparatus get bigger because the water pressure around them lessens as they rise toward the surface.

# Using Solids

Nearly all the materials we see and use every day are solids, including the homes we live in, the furniture inside our homes, all forms of transportation (from skateboards to supersonic aircraft), the food we eat, the books we read, and the clothes we wear.

Materials scientists are more concerned with solids than with the other forms of matter (liquids and gases). We can make things with solids that are strong and will keep their shape. Although solids can become liquid if enough heat energy is applied, we tend to use solid materials that stay solid under normal conditions. Imagine your surprise if this book suddenly became liquid!

Aircraft, like many other things around us, are made from materials called solids.

## Solid to liquid and back again

Sometimes we will turn solids into liquids to make them easier to shape into the forms we need. For example, molten (melted) metal can be poured into molds. Once it cools and becomes solid again, it can be put to use. Cement is mixed with water, sand, and stones to make concrete, which dries to become a tough, strong material. Concrete has many uses—for example, it is poured into place to form solid building foundations. Glass is heated and made molten to be shaped into bottles and windows.

# Solid fuels

The wide variety of fuels that we use to provide us with energy come in many forms and can be either solid, liquid, or gas. Coal, the most commonly used solid fuel, is used mainly to produce electricity. It is burned to create heat that is used to turn water into steam, which is then used to spin **turbines**, which generate electricity. Some coal is made into coke, an essential **raw material** in the production of iron and steel. Coal is also used to heat buildings and to provide energy for industrial machinery.

Wood has been used as a solid fuel for longer than any other material. Today, it is still an important fuel, particularly in developing countries, where it is used for cooking and heating. In industrialized nations such as the United States, it is no longer a major source of energy.

A blacksmith uses coke to produce the heat needed to soften iron so that it can be hammered into shape on the anvil.

# Using Liquids

Hydraulics is the study of the behavior of liquids at rest and in motion. **Civil engineers** use hydraulics to study the flow of water so that they can design water-supply systems for cities and towns, irrigation and sewage systems, and canals. **Mechanical engineers** use hydraulics to design machines such as hydraulic turbines, hydraulic brakes, power-steering for cars, controls for aircraft, and construction equipment.

## Hydraulic machines

Water pressure usually supplies the power for hydraulic machines. Some hydraulic machines, such as turbines, are driven by the force of a flowing liquid. Turbines are large wheels that use the energy of the flowing liquid to power an **electricity generator**. Turbines can also be driven by gas.

**Hydroelectric power stations use the energy of moving water to produce electricity.**

Hydraulic presses increase and transfer force through a fluid from one **piston** to a larger piston and are used for lifting heavy loads and stamping out metal parts. A simple hydraulic press consists of a fluid-filled cylinder containing two pistons, one smaller than the other. A force applied to the smaller piston is transferred through the fluid to the larger piston. The force increases in direct proportion to the ratio of the area of the larger piston to the area of the smaller piston. The brakes in a car work like hydraulic presses. Pressure on the brake pedal is transmitted through a liquid to brake pads, which press against the car's wheels.

**Pressing on the brake pedal transmits a force through the brake fluid to the brake pads, which press against the wheel.**

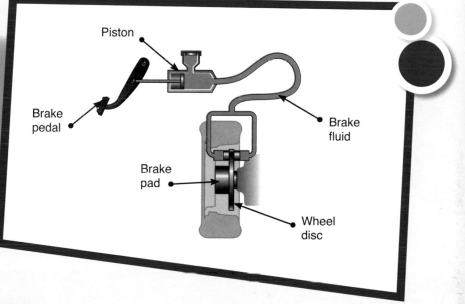

## Lubrication

Liquids such as oil or grease are used as **lubricants**. They are spread out in a thin film over the moving parts of a machine to prevent the parts from rubbing together, and so they reduce **friction**.

## Liquid fuels

Liquid fuels are easy to store and transport. They are the major source of energy for cars, aircraft, and other motorized vehicles and are also used to heat buildings.

Liquid fuels are made mainly from petroleum, also called crude oil. Most petroleum is **refined** to produce such fuels as gasoline, diesel oil, and kerosene. These fuels range in appearance from clear yellow-brown oils to thick, black tars. Gasoline is used to provide energy for most motor vehicles and propellor-engined aircraft. Diesel oil powers most trains, ships, and large trucks, while kerosene provides the energy for jet aircraft.

# Using Gases

Some gases are lighter than the **mixture** of gases that make up the air we breathe, so they will rise above it. We can use this natural lifting power to get off the ground by using balloons. Hydrogen, helium, and **natural gas** can all be used to inflate balloons. Hydrogen is the lightest of all gases and has the greatest lifting power, but it is highly **combustible** and so is not very safe. Helium is slightly heavier than hydrogen, but it does not burn and so is much safer. Natural gas produces less lift than either hydrogen or helium, but it is cheaper to produce. Gas balloons can be used for fun and for science. They have been used to carry scientific instruments 38 miles (48 kilometers) above the ground.

Hot-air balloons make good use of the fact that increasing the temperature of a gas makes it less **dense**.

## Gas refrigerator

The first practical refrigerator was built by Frenchman Ferdinand Carré in the 1850s. Ammonia gas **dissolved** in water is heated so that it boils out of the water. (Ammonia has a lower boiling point.) The ammonia moves into a **condenser**, where it cools and forms a liquid. It flows into an **evaporator**, where it vaporizes and becomes very cold. It then passes through the food compartment, cooling the food as it does so. The ammonia is dissolved in water again and flows back to the start of the cycle. Carré's refrigerator was too big for domestic use. Modern refrigerators use an electric motor (rather than gas pressure) to pump refrigerant gases called HCFCs.

## Gas fuels

Gas fuels are an efficient way of providing energy for homes and businesses. Natural gas is used to heat buildings and cook food. It consists mainly of methane, which is colorless and odorless. It is therefore usually mixed with smellier compounds so that gas leaks can be detected.

Gas turbines are used to power electricity generators, ships, and high-speed cars. They are also an important part of the engines in jet aircraft. Gas turbines burn fuels such as oil and natural gas and use the hot gases to spin the blades of the turbine.

**Gases become liquids under pressure, which allows them to be stored in convenient containers.**

## Liquids from gas

Butane and propane, which make up a small proportion of natural gas, can be turned into liquids by storing them under great pressure. When the pressure is released, they change back into gas. They are easily stored and shipped as liquids. They provide a useful portable source of fuel for people on the move or those who live far from natural gas pipelines.

# Melting and Freezing

The melting point of a substance is the temperature at which it changes from a solid to a liquid. The melting point depends partly on whether the material is a pure element, such as iron; a simple compound, such as water; or a mixture. A pure substance will melt at a definite temperature or within a narrow range of temperatures. For example, iron has a melting point of 2,795°F (1,535°C). Increasing pressure lowers the melting point of a substance.

As heat is applied to a solid such as ice, the temperature of the solid increases until it reaches its melting point (for ice, 32°F or 0°C). At this point, even though more heat is applied, the temperature will stop rising. The additional heat increases the energy of the molecules in the solid, breaking the bonds that hold them together and causing the solid to melt. The temperature will stay at the melting point until the solid has melted entirely.

The pressure of an ice skater's blade on the ice melts the ice, creating a thin film of water on the surface that allows the skater to glide along.

# Melting mixtures

Mixtures do not melt at a specific temperature. The melting point of most simple mixtures differs from that of any of the pure substances in the mixtures. Brass, an **alloy** of copper and zinc, melts over a range of 1,652°F to 1,832°F (900°C to 1,000°C), although the melting point of copper is higher than this at 1,982°F (1,083.4°C), and that of zinc is much lower at 787°F (419.6°C).

| Melting points of some common materials: | | |
|---|---|---|
| Water | 32°F | 0°C |
| Iron | 2,795°F | 1,535°C |
| Mercury | -38.2°F | -39°C |
| Oxygen | -360.4°F | -218°C |

Salting the roads in winter works because the freezing point of a liquid is lowered if something is dissolved in it.

# Freezing

Freezing is the change of a substance from a liquid to a solid—for example, when water becomes ice. The freezing point of a substance is the temperature at which this occurs. The temperature of the substance remains at this point until all the liquid has been frozen. The freezing point of a substance is the same temperature as its melting point.

The freezing point of a liquid can usually be lowered by dissolving something in it. This is why salt is scattered on pavements during icy weather. The salt dissolves in the water, lowering the temperature at which it becomes ice—and so the ice on the pavement melts.

# Boiling and Evaporation

The boiling point of a liquid is the temperature at which it changes into a gas. As the liquid is heated, the particles it consists of gain more energy, until eventually the bonds holding them together are completely broken and they fly off in all directions as a gas.

## Vapor pressure

The **vapor pressure** is the pressure produced by molecules escaping from the surface of a liquid or solid in the form of **vapor**. The greater a substance's vapor pressure, the faster it **evaporates**. The vapor pressure rises as the substance heats up. At the boiling point of a liquid, the vapor pressure is equal to the pressure of the atmosphere surrounding it. The lower the **atmospheric pressure**, the lower the temperature needed to produce a vapor pressure equal to the atmospheric pressure, and therefore the lower the boiling point.

## Melting and boiling points

Substances have different melting and boiling points because the strength of the bonds between their molecules varies. The stronger the forces of attraction between the molecules of a substance, the higher its boiling point. For example, water molecules are strongly attracted to one another and boil at 212°F (100°C). Oxygen molecules are not as strongly held together, and it therefore has a much lower boiling point of –297°F (–183°C). Some substances have especially strong bonds between their molecules and boil only at extremely high temperatures. Gold, for example, has a boiling point of 5,085°F (2,807°C).

**The boiling point of water at sea level is 212°F (100°C), but at 10,000 feet (3,050 meters) above sea level, the boiling point is about 194°F (90°C).**

# Evaporation

Evaporation is the process in which a liquid turns to a vapor without its temperature reaching the boiling point. Puddles of water left on the ground after rain eventually evaporate and disappear into the atmosphere as water vapor. At any time, a number of the molecules in a liquid will have enough energy to escape from the forces that hold the molecules together at the liquid's surface. The rate of evaporation increases if the liquid is warmed up—for example, if the Sun shines on the puddles. As the average energy of the molecules in the liquid rises, so will the number of those that have enough energy to escape.

The temperature of a liquid falls as it evaporates because the evaporating molecules remove energy from the liquid. This cooling effect is used by the body as part of its temperature control system. You cool down as sweat evaporates from your skin.

**Boiling points of some common materials:**

| | | |
|---|---|---|
| Water | 212°F | 100°C |
| Iron | 4,982°F | 2,750°C |
| Mercury | 675°F | 357°C |
| Oxygen | -297°F | -183°C |

These elephants are using the cooling effect of evaporation to stay comfortable.

# Water

Water is the most common substance on Earth. It covers 70 percent of Earth's surface and is essential to the well-being of all living organisms. It is a simple chemical compound with remarkable properties. Its chemical formula, $H_2O$, tells us that each water molecule is made up of two atoms of hydrogen and one of oxygen. At everyday temperatures, it can exist as a solid (ice), a liquid (water), or a gas (water vapor). Pure water is a colorless, odorless, tasteless liquid that freezes at 32°F (0°C) and boils at 212°F (100°C). Natural water in the environment is never pure because it always contains a variety of dissolved substances.

## Water, water everywhere

Ninety-seven percent of Earth's water is in the oceans and 2 percent is in the form of snow or ice. There is less than 1 percent available as freshwater for plants and animals.

The movement of water around Earth is called the water cycle. Water vapor in the atmosphere condenses to fall as rain, flows through rivers and streams into lakes and oceans, and is returned to the atmosphere as it evaporates.

**This shows water as a solid (ice), liquid (water), and gas (water vapor on the seal's breath)—all at the same time!**

# Water and life

Water is very important to living organisms. It helps **cells** to keep their shape and acts as a **solvent** to dissolve salts, sugars, and other substances that need to be transported around the organism. It also helps to maintain body temperature through perspiration (sweating) and evaporation.

# Properties of water

Water has unusual properties for a molecule of its size. The oxygen atom has a slight negative charge and attracts the slightly positively charged hydrogen atoms of other water molecules. The result is that bonds are formed between the water molecules, which holds them together. These bonds are called hydrogen bonds. This property also makes water a very good solvent for ionic substances, such as salts, that are formed from charged particles.

**Water's unusual properties are due to the hydrogen bonds that link its molecules together.**

Oxygen atom

Hydrogen atom

Covalent bond

Hydrogen bond

Large amounts of heat energy are needed to produce small rises in temperature in water. A great deal of heat is required to change water from its liquid state into a vapor.

In its liquid form, water cannot be **compressed**. When it is frozen, its volume expands by an eleventh. Water is most dense at 39°F (4°C). Below this temperature, the density of water decreases because the atoms of hydrogen and oxygen in a water molecule are linked at such an angle that when water becomes a solid, the molecules join up to form a crystal-like three-dimensional pattern that is less dense than water in its liquid state. This is why ice floats on water.

# Atoms in Motion

Kinetic theory is an attempt to explain the physical properties of matter in terms of the movement of the atoms and molecules that make it up. Particles of matter are never still. No matter how solid and unmoving it might appear, the molecules of the chair in which you are sitting are constantly vibrating.

## Temperature and movement

The temperature of a substance is determined by the amount of movement of the particles in it. Temperature is a measure of the average **kinetic energy** of the particles of an object. Increased temperature means increased movement. A gas is made up of rapidly moving atoms or molecules and, according to kinetic theory, it is the impact of these moving particles on a container holding the gas that accounts for the pressure of the gas.

## Chemical kinetics

Chemical kinetics is the study of the rates of **chemical reactions**. For a reaction to take place, the molecules of the elements or compounds involved in the reaction must collide with each other. They must have enough energy to break the existing chemical bonds that join the molecules together and form new ones. The amount of energy needed for a chemical reaction to take place is known as the activation energy.

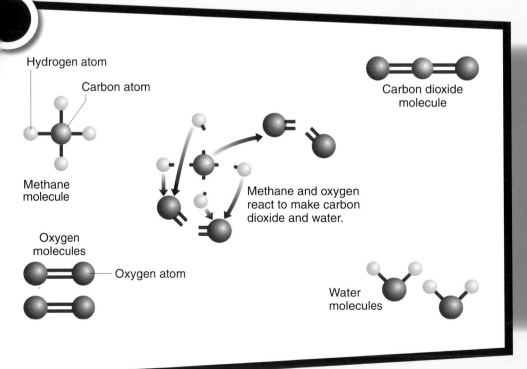

Hydrogen atom

Carbon atom

Methane molecule

Oxygen molecules

Oxygen atom

Carbon dioxide molecule

Methane and oxygen react to make carbon dioxide and water.

Water molecules

**In order for a chemical reaction to take place, the molecules have to collide with each other with sufficient energy to break the bonds that hold them together.**

# Kinetics and gases

Chemical kinetics is especially important in the study of gases. All the explanations we have about the behavior of gases come from kinetic theory, the idea of molecules in motion. Basically, all gases behave in a similar way at a specific volume, temperature, and pressure. Kinetic theory says that all gases are composed of individual molecules in continuous random motion, colliding with each other and the walls of their container and so exerting pressure on it. The actual composition of the gas is not important in kinetic theory.

When the temperature is raised, the molecules of a gas gain energy and their speed increases. Because they are now hitting the walls of the container faster and more frequently, the pressure increases, too. If more gas particles are added or if the volume of the container is reduced, the number of particles hitting the walls at any given time increases, and so the pressure also increases.

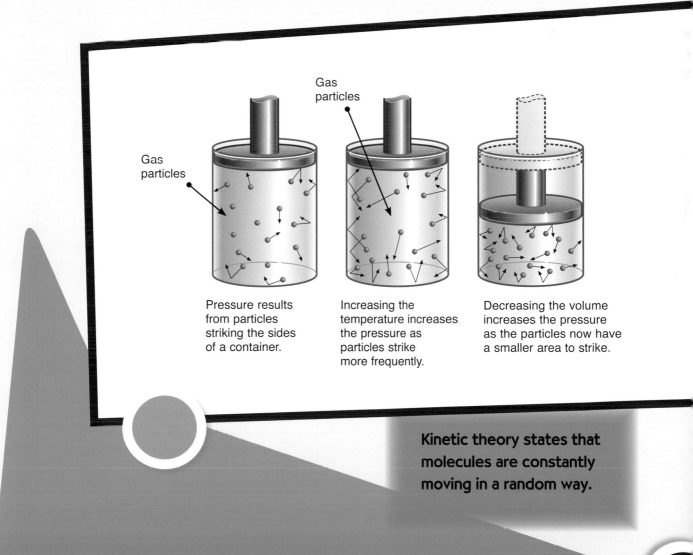

Gas particles

Gas particles

Pressure results from particles striking the sides of a container.

Increasing the temperature increases the pressure as particles strike more frequently.

Decreasing the volume increases the pressure as the particles now have a smaller area to strike.

**Kinetic theory states that molecules are constantly moving in a random way.**

# The Fourth State

In science classes, only three states of matter are commonly described. We have met them all so far:

- solids, which have a definite size and shape
- liquids, which have a definite volume and no definite shape
- gases, which have no definite size or shape.

What happens if we continue to raise the temperature of a gas? If the temperature is raised to over 18,032°F (10,000°C), the molecules of the gas begin to collide with each other so violently that the bonds that hold them together are broken and they split into individual atoms. Negatively charged electrons are knocked off the atoms, which now have a positive charge. Charged atoms are called ions. Some atoms may remain completely intact, and so a gas mixture—consisting of ions, electrons, and neutral atoms—is produced. This mixture is called a plasma.

Nucleus of atom

Electron

**A plasma contains atoms, electrons, and ions.**

## Electric plasma

All these charged particles mean that a plasma is a good **conductor** of electricity. Apart from being very hot, a plasma differs from a gas because a plasma's movements are affected by electric and **magnetic fields**. In fact, the ions and the electrons in a plasma form an electric **current**, which in turn produces a magnetic field. The fact that a plasma can generate electric and magnetic fields, and is in turn affected by them, makes it behave in a way that is quite unlike any of the other three states of matter. The number of electrons and ions in the plasma are equal. So, although it has magnetic and electrical properties, overall a plasma is neutral.

# Looking for plasmas

Plasmas exist in the hot centers of stars. The Sun is a huge ball of plasma, heated by **nuclear reactions** at its core. The tails of comets are partly made of plasma from gases **ionized** by the energy of the Sun. Above Earth's atmosphere, matter exists in the plasma state in the magnetosphere, the magnetic field that surrounds Earth. Plasma in the magnetosphere is largely responsible for shielding Earth from cosmic **radiation**. Plasmas can also be found closer to home. Lightning can be thought of as a massive electrical discharge in the atmosphere that produces a plasma. When an electric current is passed through neon gas in a neon light, it produces light and plasma.

## Plasma energy

In an attempt to harness the fusion energy of stars here on Earth, physicists are studying devices that create and confine very hot plasmas in magnetic fields.

In a plasma, atoms are stripped of electrons, forming a "soup" of charged particles.

# Glossary

**alloy** mixture of two or more metals or a metal and a nonmetal

**atmospheric pressure** weight of gases in the air pressing against something

**atom** tiny particle from which all materials are made; the smallest part of an element that can exist

**bond** force that holds atoms together in molecules

**brittle** describes a substance that is hard, but that will break or shatter easily

**capillary** very thin tube

**cell** smallest building block of living things

**charged** having an electric charge

**chemical reaction** reaction that takes place between two or more substances in which energy is given out or taken in and new substances are produced

**civil engineer** engineer who designs roads, bridges, and similar structures

**combustible** capable of catching fire

**compound** substance that is made up of atoms of two or more elements

**compressed** flattened by pressure or squeezed into a smaller space

**condensation point** temperature at which a gas becomes a liquid

**condenser** piece of apparatus for condensing a gas (changing it to a liquid)

**conductor** something that conducts heat or electricity

**covalent** type of bond formed between atoms in which the atoms share electrons

**crystal** solid in which the atoms are arranged in a regular pattern

**current** flow of something, such as a liquid, gas, or electric charge

**dense** describes a substance in which the atoms or molecules from which it is made are packed closely together

**dissolve** become incorporated into a liquid and form a solution

**electricity generator** machine for generating electricity

**electron** negatively charged particle that is found in all atoms and that is the main carrier of electrical energy

**element** substance that cannot be broken down into simpler substances by chemical reactions. An element is made up of just one type of atom.

**evaporate** change into a vapor or a gas

**evaporator** piece of apparatus in which evaporation takes place

**fluid** substance that has no fixed shape; a gas or a liquid

**friction** force that acts to slow down or stop objects that are moving against each other

**fusion** when two small atoms combine to make a larger atom with the release of a great deal of energy

**gravity** force of attraction between objects

**ion** atom or group of atoms that has an electric charge

**ionic** type of bond between atoms in which electrons are transferred from one atom to another

**ionized** describes an atom or molecule that has gained or lost electrons and so has an overall electric charge

**kinetic energy** energy of movement

**latent heat** heat taken in or given out when a substance changes from one state to another

**lubricant** substance that is used to reduce friction between the moving parts of a machine

**macromolecule** molecule containing a very large number of atoms

**magnetic field** pattern of magnetic influence around a magnet

**mass** amount of matter that something contains

**mechanical engineer** engineer who designs and constructs machines

**mixture** material made of different substances mixed together, but not combined chemically

**molecule** two or more atoms combined together. If the atoms are the same, it is an element; if they are different, it is a compound.

**natural gas** gas that comes from the earth. It is used as a fuel and raw material.

**neutron** one of the fundamental components of an atom, found in the atom's nucleus. A neutron has no electric charge.

**nuclear reaction** reaction that involves changes to atoms

**particle** tiny portion of matter

**physics** science that deals with the facts about matter and motion

**piston** disc or cylinder that moves up and down inside a tube

**pressure** force pushing on a given area

**proton** one of the fundamental components of an atom, found in the atom's nucleus. A proton has a positive electric charge.

**radiation** high energy rays or particles. Cosmic radiation comes from space.

**raw material** material used in the manufacture of something

**refine** have impurities removed

**solvent** substance that can dissolve something

**sublimation** changing from a solid to a gas

**surface tension** force in the surface of a liquid produced by the molecules at the surface being pulled by those below them

**turbine** motor with a set of blades that rotate when pushed by a moving stream of liquid or gas

**vapor** type of gas

**vapor pressure** pressure produced by a liquid as it evaporates

**vaporization** converting into a vapor or gas

**volume** amount of space occupied by something

# Further Information

Oxlade, Chris. *States of Matter*. Chicago: Heinemann Library, 2007.

Snedden, Robert. *Changing Materials*. Chicago: Heinemann Library, 2008.

Stille, Darlene R. *Matter and Material*. Chanhassen, Minn.: Child's World, 2005.

Walker, Sally M. *Matter*. Minneapolis: Lerner, 2006.

# Index